# READING
## FOR DETAIL

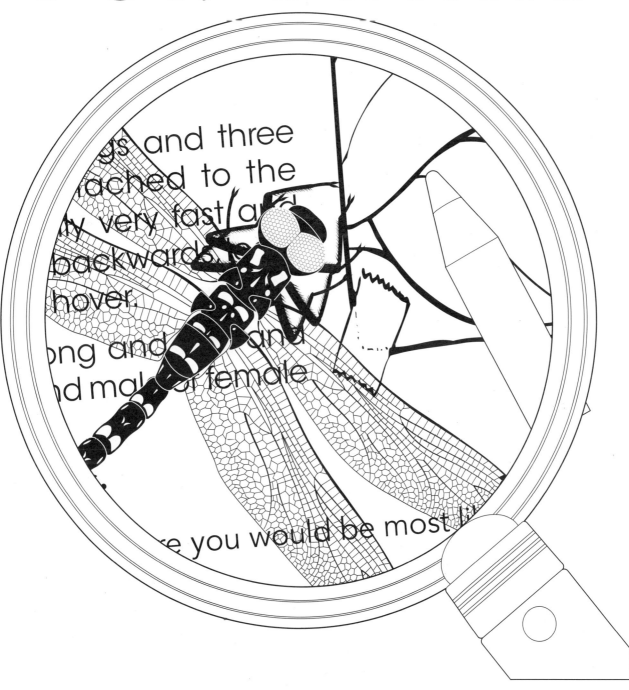

Published by World Teachers Press®

Published with the permission of R.I.C. Publications Pty. Ltd.

Copyright © 2001 by Didax, Inc., Rowley, MA 01969.  All rights reserved.

First published by R.I.C. Publications Pty. Ltd., Perth, Western Australia.  Revised by Didax Educational Resources.

Printed in the United States of America.

Order Number 2-5183
ISBN 1-58324-117-5

A B C D E F 03 02 01

Educational Resources
395 Main Street
Rowley, MA 01969
www.worldteacherspress.com

# Teachers Notes

Activities include:
- word study (finding antonyms, synonyms, dictionary meanings, etc.)
- short-answer questions
- cause and effect
- retrieval charts
- points of view
- highlighting specific details

*Reading for Detail* can be used in a variety of situations, depending on the reading level of individual students.

## 1. Whole class

- Each student will require their own copy of the text and activities.
- Introduce the title and theme of the text.
- Teacher can read the text while students follow

  or

  individual students can have turns in reading sections of the text.
- The text can then be discussed orally with teacher guidance.
- Activities can be carefully explained to the students before they commence writing their own answers.

## 2. Independently

- Students who are capable readers can read the text and complete the activities on their own.
- Each student will again require their own copy.

## 3. Small group

- While capable students are working independently, the teacher can select a small group of students who need more one-to-one guidance.
- The pages can be treated as in the whole-class approach. Certain students may need more help in completing the answers.

# The Trojan Horse

 ong, long ago one of the greatest cities in the ancient world was Troy. It was surrounded by mighty walls which kept the people who lived inside safe from enemies. This legendary city was ruled by King Priam who had a son, Paris.

One day Paris traveled to Greece to visit the Greek king, Menelaus. Menelaus's wife, Helen, was supposedly the most beautiful woman in the world. Paris fell in love with her and, after much pleading, he persuaded her to come and live with him in Troy.

Consequently, Menelaus was furious and declared war on Paris and the people of Troy. The Greeks armed themselves with weapons and, led by their bravest heroes, set sail for Troy. And so the Trojan war began.

This terrible war was to last 10 years. The Greeks tried again and again but could not capture Troy. The colossal stone walls prevented successful attempts to gain entry. Both sides lost many great warriors.

As warriors continued to die, no one seemed any closer to winning the war. Finally, one of the Greek heroes, Odysseus, had an idea. He ordered workers to build a huge wooden horse, in which some Greek warriors hid. The rest of the Greeks then pretended to sail away. The horse was left standing outside the city walls.

When the Trojans saw the Greek ships leaving they were overjoyed and flung open the city gates. The curious Trojans dragged the massive horse inside the city to look at it more closely. That night there was a great celebration in Troy, with feasts and dancing. Afterwards, when the city was sleeping soundly, the warriors crept out of the horse and let in the rest of the Greeks, who had returned in the ships during the night.

The Greeks attacked the people of Troy and burned the city. Very few Trojans escaped. Paris was one of the many Trojan warriors killed in the war. Helen was taken back home to King Menelaus.

And so the Trojan war ended.

## Answer these questions.

**1.** Write another title for this legend.

_____

**2.** Highlight,   (a) what a person who came from Troy was called.

                (b) what a person who came from Greece was called.

**3.** Circle adjectives from the passage that mean big or strong.

**4.** Complete a brief summary of events that happened in the legend.

King Priam's son, Paris, traveled from Troy to Greece to visit King Menelaus.

Helen was returned to Troy.

**5.** A famous saying developed from this legend. Using your knowledge of the legend, explain what you think the saying means.

The face that launched a thousand ships. _____

_____

_____

**6.** (a)  Explain what the word "revenge" means.

_____

_____

(b)  War can be caused by revenge.
Give an example of this in the legend.

_____

_____

**7.** At the time of this war, people used a "herald" to announce important news. There were no newspapers of course! Write the brief announcement the herald might call out to tell of the Greek triumph.

_____

_____

_____

# The Elephant's Child

Long ago, elephants had short noses, not trunks. One of these elephants lived in Africa. He was called the Elephant's Child, because he was the youngest in his family. He was also the most curious, and was always asking questions.

One day, he asked, "What does the crocodile eat?"

No one knew the answer. The wise Kolokolo bird, however, told him what he should do.

"Go to the Limpopo River," he said, "and you will find out."

So the next morning, the Elephant's Child set out on the long journey to the river, even though he didn't even know what a crocodile looked like. When he reached the banks of the Limpopo River, he walked along until he met an animal that looked to him like a log.

"Have you seen a crocodile anywhere?" asked the Elephant's Child.

"I am a crocodile," was the reply.

The Elephant's Child was excited, and asked him, "What do you eat?"

"Come close," said the crocodile, "and I'll tell you."

The Elephant's Child started to kneel down, when suddenly the crocodile grabbed him by the nose with his teeth, calling out, "Today, I will start with an elephant!"

But the Elephant's Child was not easy for the crocodile to drag straight into the water. While the crocodile pulled as hard as he could, the Elephant's Child stood his ground, and also pulled as hard as he could. As this happened, his nose began to stretch.

A python watching nearby helped by knotting himself around the Elephant's Child's legs and pulling as well. The Elephant's Child's nose kept on stretching. With both the Elephant's Child and the python pulling, it became too much for the crocodile. He finally let go, and disappeared into the Limpopo.

The Elephant's Child's nose was now as long as an elephant's is today. He waited for days for it to shrink, but when it would not, he decided to go home.

On his way home, he discovered that he could do some amazing things with his new nose. He could swat insects, pick up things to eat and throw mud all over himself to keep cool.

When he got home, his family was impressed with what he could do with his long nose. When the Elephant's Child told them he got it from the crocodile, they all rushed off to the Limpopo to get one too. And that's the reason why elephants have long trunks.

**Answer these questions.**

1. Highlight the sentence the crocodile said to fool the Elephant's Child.

2. Circle the amazing things the Elephant's Child could do with his new trunk. Write one more thing he might be able to do.

_____

**3.** The crocodile decides to advertise his skill of stretching trunks in the *Elephant Trumpeter*. Write his advertisement, including details like location, procedure, healing time, advantages and payment.

**4.** For each answer below, write a matching question.

QUESTION                                ANSWER

(a) _____    To find out what a crocodile eats.

(b) _____    He knotted himself around the Elephant Child's legs.

(c) _____    "Today, I will start with an elephant!"

(d) _____    They all rushed off to the Limpopo.

**5.** Write a new ending for the story, starting from, "When he got home …"

_____

_____

_____

_____

# April Fools' Feast

Another salad sandwich lurking in my box
And porridge every morning, just like Goldilocks
I'm tired of eating healthy food that tastes like knitted socks

Today is April Fools' Day, so I'll make a little treat
A feast that will fool everyone, something really neat
Let's see what's in the kitchen that tastes sickly sweet

I'll need some ice cream, cookie crumbs, a long thin candy bar
And some lovely chocolate topping—I think I'll take the jar
Then in a bag and off to school, riding in the car

I'll fool the whole class with my feast, they won't believe it's true
When gravy, mashed potato and a crunchy fish stick too
Turns out to be a sweet surprise—a feast fit for a fool!

**Answer these questions.**

1. Check fact or opinion.

    (a)  The girl was sick of healthy food.

    (b)  The girl often did these tricks.

    (c)  April Fools' Day is a time for playing tricks.

    (d)  The class was going to fall for the trick.

    (e)  She had porridge for breakfast every day.

| Fact | Opinion |
|---|---|
|  |  |
|  |  |
|  |  |
|  |  |
|  |  |

2. Choose one of the words below to replace the last word from this part of the poem. Then write a rhyming word for the second line.

    meal          snack          feast          lunch

    Today is April Fools' Day, so I'll make a little treat _____

    A feast that will fool everyone, something _____

**3.** Why was the girl going to make the trick meal?

_____

_____

**4.** (a) Write what you think the girl might say to a classmate to convince him or her that meal is mashed potato, gravy and a fish stick.

    (b) Write the classmate's reply.

**5.** Do you think the girl's plan will succeed? _____

Why/Why not? _____

_____

_____

**6.** Match what each ingredient in the trick meal was supposed to look like.

| Real food | Trick food |
|---|---|
| ice cream | |
| chocolate topping | |
| candy bar and cookie crumbs | |

**7.** Write a synonym from the poem for these words and phrases.

    (a) hiding

    _____

    (b) deceive

    _____

    (c) syrup

    _____

    (d) nutritious

    _____

# The Clock Struck

**Characters**: Grace, Tom, Sally

**Scene**: The family room

*Grace is sitting on the floor, writing a letter. An open box sits next to her. Her older brother and sister enter and startle her with their first words. They talk to her in teasing voices.*

| | |
|---|---|
| **TOM** | Whatcha doing, Grace? |
| **SALLY** | Mom said you got a package in the mail. |
| **TOM** | Who's it from? |
| **SALLY** | What is it? |
| **GRACE** | It's from Uncle Albert, and it's something very special … (*Sally reaches into the box and pulls out a bright yellow clock, which is ticking loudly. It has 4 buttons on the top—red, orange, green and gold.*) Hey, give it back! |
| **SALLY** | A clock! What a stupid present! Still, that's what you'd expect from the weirdest uncle in the world. |
| **TOM** | Funny how he sends it to the second weirdest person in the world. (*They both laugh.*) |
| **GRACE** | I'm asking you one more time to give it back, or you'll be sorry. (*They both ignore her.*) |
| **SALLY** | Wait, there's a tag on it. (*Reads aloud*) "Dear Grace, I hope you find this useful. I have made the changes you suggested. Please let me know what you think. Love, Uncle Albert." |
| **TOM** | Useful? How could a clock be useful? He really is weird. (*He takes the clock from Sally. The orange button begins to flash.*) What's this supposed to do? (*He presses the button, and the clock begins ticking slowly*). Oh dear, looks like I've broken it. Sorry, Grace, guess it wasn't so useful after all. (*Suddenly, Tom gives a shudder. He starts to move and talk in slow motion.*) |
| **TOM** | Hey, what's going on? |
| **SALLY** | Tom, stop fooling around. |
| **TOM** | I can't help it. |
| **SALLY** | Give it here. (*She snatches it from Tom, who immediately goes back to normal.*) |
| **GRACE** | I wouldn't do that if I were you. |
| **SALLY** | Why, do you think I might break your precious clock? (*The green button flashes.*) What's this do? (*The clock begins to tick quickly. Sally starts to talk and move in fast motion.*) |
| **SALLY** | Somebody help me! Grace, take it back, take it back! (*She throws the clock to Grace, who catches it neatly. The clock begins to tick at a normal pace.*) (*Sally and Tom start to look frightened.*) |

| | |
|---|---|
| **TOM** | Just what have you and Uncle Albert been up to? |
| **SALLY** | What are you doing to us? |
| **GRACE** | I don't know what you're talking about. <br> (*The red button begins to flash. Grace smiles, and goes to press it.*) |
| **SALLY/ TOM** | Don't do that! <br> (*Grace calmly puts the clock on the floor.*) |
| **GRACE** | Perhaps you'd better press it. It might make everything stop. <br> (*Sally and Tom race to the clock together, press the button and both immediately freeze.*) |
| **GRACE** | (*smiling*) Now that was a silly thing to do. (*She dusts off her hands, and picks up the letter she was writing before. She reads it aloud.*) |
| **GRACE** | "Dear Uncle Albert, Thanks for all your hard work. I'm glad you acted on my suggestions, particularly regarding the red button—it worked just as I planned. Will write soon, love from Grace." <br> (*She strolls over to Sally and Tom, who are still frozen. She taps her pen on the paper thoughtfully, then writes as she speaks.*) |
| **GRACE** | "I haven't had a chance yet to experiment with the final feature you added, but I am very eager to try it out. Luckily, I have two willing volunteers who love danger." <br> (*The gold button begins to flash. She smiles, and her finger comes down to touch it.*) <br> <br> I hope you like dinosaurs. |
| CURTAIN. | Ticking stops. |

Tick
Tick
Tick . . .

## Answer these questions.

**1.** Highlight the part when Tom and Sally first begin to suspect the clock is unusual.

**2.** This play is called "The Clock Struck." Write another suitable title for the play.

_____

**3.** Re-read the last half of the play. Write what you think happens to Tom and Sally when the ticking stops.

_____

_____

_____

_____

**4.** (a) Write two questions you would like to ask Uncle Albert about Grace and the clock.

_____

_____

(b) Draw what you think Uncle Albert looks like.

**5.** Imagine you are Grace. Explain why you wanted Uncle Albert to make the clock.

_____

_____

_____

**6.** The clock ticks throughout the play in different ways and then stops at the end. Why do you think the playwright had this happen?

_____

_____

_____

# Animal Camouflage

**Did you know ...**

Camouflage is a kind of disguise that makes something hard to see against its surroundings. Many animals are camouflaged by the colors and patterns of their skin, scales, fur, or feathers. Camouflage helps an animal to survive.

Both hunting and hunted animals use camouflage. Predators that catch other creatures are camouflaged so they can creep up on their prey. A lioness has tawny-colored fur to mix in with the soil and grasslands of Africa. She can slowly creep up to her prey without being seen. Hunted animals, such as rabbits, have fur that blends in with the earth and grass. A rabbit can look almost invisible—unless it moves!

Another type of camouflage is "disruptive coloration." Animals with spots, stripes, or patches are difficult to see against the background. An example is the zebra. Its stripes make it hard to see in the dim light of dawn and dusk. During the day, it is difficult for a predator to pick out a single zebra because the entire herd has similar stripes.

A lizard called a chameleon has an amazing ability—it can change color! Its eyes pick up the colors of its surroundings. The brain sends signals along nerves to the pigment or color cells of the skin. The color changes occur within seconds.

Some animals have warning coloration. The female red-back spider has a poisonous bite. Her red back reminds or warns others to avoid her. Some harmless creatures also do this. An example is the wasp-fly. It is colored like a wasp, but does not have the harmful sting.

Some animals pretend to be part of a plant, such as a flower, leaf, or twig. In this way they can hide from predators or hide from a creature they wish to catch. Frogs and toads are experts at this. A tree frog is perfectly colored to match the leaves where it lives. It can hide from enemies, or, if an insect comes too close to its hiding place, it can flick out its tongue and catch it.

**Answer these questions.**

**1.** Highlight an interesting fact from each section of the report.

**2.** Find an antonym in the report for these words or phrases.

(a)  prey  _____

(b)  lion  _____

(c)  harmless  _____

(d)  bright  _____

(e)  easily seen  _____

(f)  dusk  _____

**3.** Write key words and phrases to describe how each of these animals uses camouflage.

| Animal | Camouflage |
|---|---|
| lioness | |
| zebra | |
| chameleon | |
| tree frog | |

**4.** Complete the questions to match the answer.

Answer:  She has a poisonous bite.

Question:          How does the _____?

Answer:  The wasp-fly.

Question:          What kind of _____?

Answer:  Camouflage

Question:          What does the _____?

**5.** Write words or phrases from the report that describe different ways animals are camouflaged.

# Carnivorous Plant Facts

You will probably have heard of the word "carnivore" (or "carnivorous") before. It means to eat meat. But, how can a plant eat meat? Plants don't have teeth!

Of course, you won't see a carnivorous plant biting into a juicy piece of steak or a chicken drumstick! Carnivorous plants usually eat meat in the form of insects or insect larvae. These plants attract, capture, kill and digest animal life forms. Each type of plant has a different way of doing these things but all have those four common traits. There are more than 500 different species of carnivorous plants.

## Did you know ...

Carnivorous plants digest their prey by the use of special enzymes. After the prey has been digested, all that remains is a mass of leftover crunchy bits!

The Venus flytrap is probably the most famous of all carnivorous plants. It can trap insects in its leaves. The leaves are actually traps which the plant holds open in the air, like a clamshell. Insects are attracted to the plant by sweet nectar. When one lands on a leaf or "trap" it snaps shut. Each "trap" lasts for about three meals then dies.

Pitcher plants have trumpet-shaped leaves that collect rainwater. Sweet substances around the rim of each "trumpet" attract insects to the plant. Insects enter and drown in the rainwater.

Insects are lured to the sundew by sweet nectar. The leaves of a sundew plant grows hairs that give off a sticky substance. When an insect gets stuck on the substance the hairs wrap around it. Eventually the insect suffocates and is digested.

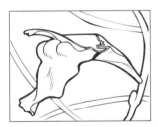

A bladderwort mostly grows underwater. They have hundreds of little flask-shaped bladders on their stems and leaves. Large yellow or purplish flowers attract insects such as mosquitoes. When the insect touches the sensitive hairs around the bladder's mouth, the sides spring outward and the insect is pulled inside and trapped.

Not all carnivorous plants are small. Some species can grow to 20 meters in length as climbing vines. They have been known to eat creatures as large as frogs!

## Answer these questions.

1. Highlight the sentence that gives an accurate definition of all carnivorous plants.

2. In one sentence, describe how a carnivorous plant can digest its prey.

_____

_____

_____

**3.** Complete the chart with facts about each carnivorous plant.

| | How the plant attracts the insect | How the insect is trapped by the plant |
|---|---|---|
| Venus flytrap | | |
| Pitcher plant | | |
| Sundew | | |
| Bladderwort | | |

**4.** Use a dictionary to find the meaning of the word "pitcher" and explain how the plant got its name.

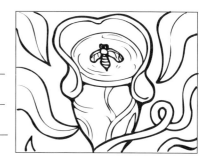

_____

_____

_____

**5.** Write an antonym from the fact sheet for these words.

(a) sour _____ (b) herbivore _____

(c) release _____ (d) repel _____

**6.** Draw your own carnivorous plant. Use a mixture of the features you have read about. Label and describe each part.

# A Snack for Shannon

"Mom, I'm home!" Shannon called, dumping her schoolbag in the middle of the floor. "May I have something to eat?"

"Hello, darling," Mom called back from upstairs. "There's plenty of fruit in the fridge."

"Don't want fruit!" Shannon answered rudely. "Can't I have something else? Like a sandwich?"

"Shannon, you heard me," her mother warned. "It's fruit or nothing! Every time you make one of your famous sandwiches, you end up not eating dinner because you're too full!"

Shannon stamped her foot angrily—but not too loudly, in case Mom heard! She wasn't going to eat fruit. Mom was upstairs in her office working, so Shannon could eat what she wanted.

There was nothing very exciting in the fridge—just a lot of fruit like Mom said—so she had a look in the pantry. Ahh! This was more like it! There were crackers and sweet biscuits, and . . . she spotted a small gold-colored can almost hidden behind the other groceries. On tiptoes she reached in and grabbed it.

When she saw the word "sardines" on the lid, she didn't read any further. Sardines were her absolute favorite! She opened the can and spread the contents on top of six big crackers.

Ummm! They were yummy! In no time, the crackers had gone, and Shannon wiped her finger around the inside of the tin to get the last little pieces out.

She was so busy, she never heard the footsteps behind her until a voice said, "Shannon! What are you doing?"

Before Shannon could even begin to answer, Mom saw the can in her hand.

"I thought I told you only fruit!" she said. "Well, perhaps *this* will help you to remember in future." She took the tin out of Shannon's hand. "You didn't even read the label did you?"

"Yes I did," Shannon said. "It says 'Sardines'."

"It also says 'Cat food only'," Mom said. "I almost hope it gives you a tummy ache for being so naughty. Now pick up your bag and go straight to your room while I decide what to do with you."

Shannon threw her schoolbag on her bed. She didn't feel the least bit sick. In fact, she had a sudden urge to lick her lips, several times, to enjoy the taste of the sardines.

She wasn't going to have any tummy aches, either. Just because it was cat food didn't make the tiniest bit of difference. Mom was just plain wrong.

Shannon sat on her bed, licked her hand, and began to wash carefully behind her ears.

**Answer these questions.**

**1.** Write another title that suits the story.

_____

**2.** Imagine the story continues after the last sentence.

Write the next sentence. _____

_____

**3.** Each time something happens in the story, it causes an effect on the characters. Write an effect for each cause below.

| Cause | Effect |
|---|---|
| (a) Shannon didn't want to eat fruit, so … | she _____ _____ |
| (b) Shannon was so busy eating … | she _____ _____ |
| (c) Mom caught Shannon eating cat food, so … | _____ _____ |
| (d) Because Shannon ate cat food, she … | _____ _____ |

4. Do you think anything would have happened if Shannon had eaten fruit? Why/Why not?

_____

_____

5. Circle the best answer for the questions below.

(a) Shannon ate the sardines …

    (i)    in a sandwich.

    (ii)   with some fruit.

    (iii)  on crackers.

    (iv)  from a plate.

(b) Mom was cross because …

    (i)    Shannon ate cat food.

    (ii)   Shannon disobeyed her.

    (iii)  Shannon ate some fruit.

    (iv)  Shannon turned into a cat.

# Helping Mom and Dad

"Mom, can I invite Brett over to stay tomorrow night, please? It's Friday, and we don't have any homework. Can I, please?"

Mom was sitting at the kitchen table, peeling potatoes. Dad was asleep next to her, resting his head on his arms, which were folded on the table. Mom put down her peeler and looked at James. She could see he wanted so badly to have his friend over.

"I'm so sorry, James," she said sadly. "I don't think that's such a good idea."

"But why, Mom?" James asked, almost in tears. "I'm never allowed to have friends come to the house? Why, Mom?"

"Come here, son," Mom said, holding out her arms. James went to her and she hugged him close.

"I know it's hard for you," Mom said softly. "But I'm just worried other people might think we're a little … strange. And then they would tease you and make fun of you."

"No they wouldn't, Mom," James protested. "We're not strange at all, we're just ordinary people."

Mom sighed heavily. "To tell you the truth, James, I really don't feel well enough to have visitors to stay. My neck has been so stiff and sore lately it's given me a splitting headache. And your poor father—he's so rundown. He really needs a good rest. Just look at him!"

"I can help, Mom!" James said. "Honestly! I know just what to do. If I can make you and Dad feel better, can Brett come over? Please?"

"Well . . . ," his mom said.

"Great! Thanks, Mom!" James almost shouted. "Just sit there, don't move." He rushed over to the kitchen drawer and rummaged around inside, then come running back to stand behind his mother as soon as he had found what he needed—two wrenches.

"Hang on, Mom," he said. "This won't take a second." A minute later he said, "There! How does that feel?"

Mom moved her head from side to side. "Oh, James," she said, "That's much better! How did you do it?"

"Easy," James said proudly. "Dad had tightened your bolts too much! I just loosened them up a bit!"

"What about your father? Can you help him?"

"Sure thing!" James said. He ran over to the kitchen bench and yanked the power cord out of the toaster. Leaving it plugged into the socket, he reached across, lifted up his father's hair at the back of his neck, and plugged the power cord into Dad's head. Then he turned the power on. Dad opened his eyes and sat up immediately.

"He just let his battery run too low, that's all," James said. "Shall I tell Brett to come over straight after school tomorrow?"

## Answer these questions

**1.** Highlight the part where you first know for sure the family is unusual.

**2.** Write a question you would like to ask James.

**3.** What excuses does Mom give James for not wanting Brett to stay over?

_____

_____

_____

_____

_____

_____

_____

**4.** From the description given, draw James fixing his Mom's headache.

**5.** Find the adjective or adverb from the story to complete these phrases. Next to each, rewrite the phrase with another word that makes sense.

(a) Mom sighed _____      _____

(b) _____ headache      _____

(c) _____ rest      _____

(d) Mom said _____      _____

**6.** The beginning and end of the story are written below in the bread of the toasted sandwich. Write the filling (middle of the story).

James asked if Brett could stay over.

_____

_____

_____

_____

_____

James was going to tell Brett he could stay over.

# Crushing Blow

By Anthea Hill

A large nest of bull ants was in shock yesterday as the ants struggled to come to terms with a crushing accident that injured thousands of their family and friends.

The ant nest, long established in a popular picnic area, was stepped on by an unthinking human. The teenage boy, seemingly unaware of the damage he had caused, strode away, laughing with his friends.

"It all happened so fast," said the bull ant Queen. "It was a normal working day, when suddenly the sun seemed to go out, and the shadow of a giant shoe came down towards us. There was just no time for some ants to get out of the way."

Army ants immediately rushed to help, but despite their speedy response, there was little they could do to help the injured.

**"It all happened so fast …
There was just no time
for some ants to
get out of the way."**
— Queen

"Our hospital is overflowing," said a doctor. "We respect the fact that humans use the picnic area as well; after all, they supply us with many tasty crumbs. But the cost to our community is enormous."

One of the injured ants was well-known actor Anthony Thorax. Upon hearing the news, the hospital

Anthony Thorax after his release from hospital.

was inundated with concerned fans, who waited patiently throughout the night for news of their hero.

A statement was released late yesterday saying Anthony was touched by the thoughtfulness of all his fans, and he would be heading home soon.

The Queen is considering moving the ant nest, but, despite the large number of devastating incidents involving humans which occur regularly throughout the year, many in the community do not want to shift from the place that has been the only home they have ever known.■

## Answer these questions.

**1.** Write another catchy headline for this article.

_____

_____

**2.** Fill in the missing words.

(a) _____ of ants were injured.

(b) The ants thought of the _____ boy as an _____ human.

(c) Among the injured was a _____ actor.

(d) So many were injured that the _____ was _____.

**3.** Fill in the information about the newspaper report.

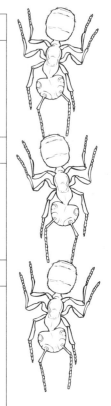

| Who? | What? |
|---|---|
| | |
| **When?** | **Why?** |
| | |
| **How?** | |
| | |

**4.** The next day Anthony Thorax was interviewed by the *Bull Ant Bulletin*. He was only too pleased to hear the sound of his own voice and gave a most elaborate account of what happened to him.

Write his account.

_____

_____

_____

_____

_____

_____

_____

**5.** The Queen is considering moving the ant nest. Write points for and against this decision.

| For | Against |
|---|---|
| | |

# Deluxe Dinner Parties

*Belinda George*
*22 Fisher Street*
*HILL VIEW*

*The Manager*
*Deluxe Dinner Parties*
*PO Box 778*
*SIMPSON POINT*

*Dear Sir:*

*I am writing to complain about the service I received recently from your company. Your motto is supposed to be "We do it all"—but this was far from my experience.*

*I contacted you a week ago concerning a special dinner party I wanted to hold at my home for eight people. On the phone, you assured me that your staff would make it a "night to remember." Well, they certainly did, but not for the reasons I had hoped.*

*Last night, the waiters and chef I hired from you were supposed to turn up at 6:00 p.m. sharp, a full hour before my guests arrived. They arrived instead at 6:45 p.m., with no apology offered. They were the scruffiest bunch of catering professionals I had ever seen, with no sign of the smart uniforms you have in your glossy brochures. One of them even had jeans on!*

*When they began to prepare the food, I noticed that the main course was not the grilled fish I ordered from your menu, but instead was roast beef. As one of my guests does not eat red meat, this was very embarrassing.*

*The entree was not ready by the time my guests arrived, and we had to wait for over an hour to start dinner. When it was finally ready, the soup was not hot, but lukewarm. The beef was undercooked, and the chocolate mousse was bitter. The service of the waiters, which you claim is "professional and unobtrusive," was shocking—they were loud, clumsy and generally irritating.*

*After such a disappointing meal, I had hoped your staff would at least leave the kitchen "spick and span," as you advertised, but they left as soon as we had drunk our coffees, leaving a total mess. Your staff were not even discreet in asking for their money; they demanded it in front of all the guests.*

*To say that I am unimpressed is putting it mildly. You say in your brochure that you have a money-back guarantee if your customers are not satisfied; well, I am demanding my money back, as well as an apology from your sad excuse for a catering business.*

*I look forward to hearing from you soon.*

*BELINDA GEORGE*

## Answer these questions.

**1.** Highlight everything that went wrong.

**2.** Write one thing Belinda didn't complain about.

_____

_____

**3.** Design the Deluxe Dinner Parties brochure that Belinda might have read before booking her dinner party. Use quotes from the letter as well as your own ideas.

**4.** Write four things that Belinda complains about.
Next to each, write an excuse the Manager might give for why things went wrong.

| Belinda's Complaint | Manager's Excuse |
|---|---|
| (a) The staff turned up late. | Their car broke down. |
| (b) _____ | _____ |
| (c) _____ | _____ |
| (d) _____ | _____ |
| (e) _____ | _____ |

**5.** Do you think Belinda's money should be refunded? _____

Why/Why not? _____

_____

_____

_____

# The Secret Diary of the Monster in the Bedroom

Dear Diary,

Another full night's work last night. I'm really getting fed up with the job now. I'm tired of dust under beds and in closets, getting a sore throat from growling and squeaking and, most of all, frightening little kids just for the money. I'm beginning to feel guilty, and that means I'm not doing my job properly. If the boss knew, he'd be really angry. He's been the Bogeyman for years, and is responsible for many kids' nightmares.

I guess I'll just have to accept that I'm not much of a monster. Take last night for instance. It started out all right. I hid under a little girl's bed and made scratching noises. Almost straightaway she called out for her parents and they switched on the light to show her there was nothing there. Of course there wasn't—I'd made myself invisible. (Parents! They should believe their kids.) I was feeling pleased with myself, but after they left, I felt sorry for the little girl, so I left her some candy under her pillow. I hope she might think they're from a fairy.

It all went downhill from there. At the next house, I cast some scary-looking shadows on the ceiling, but when the boy began to look frightened, I felt bad, so I made some clown shadows instead. He really liked those! He smiled and went off to sleep. And I'm supposed to be a monster!

Also, the days are quite boring, with nothing much to do. Oh sure, I'm still doing what the boss wants—hiding things from the family like keys and library books, and taking socks from the washing machine. But my heart's just not in it anymore.

I'm going to leave and find a newer, nicer job—maybe an elf for Santa or the tooth fairy's assistant. I'm not sure yet. But I'm not going to give up until I find something. Somebody must want a kind monster like me.

**Answer these questions.**

1. Highlight the two nice things the monster did.

2. Circle four verbs that tell what the monster did.

**3.** In one or two sentences describe what the monster is talking about in each paragraph.

| Paragraph | Summary |
|---|---|
| 1. | |
| 2. | |
| 3. | |
| 4. | |
| 5. | |

**4.** The monster has decided to give up his job. The Bogeyman now has to advertise for somebody else. Help him to write the advertisement. Include:

- the hours of work
- job description
- skills required

Monster Weekly

### Positions Vacant

Monster required ...

# Diary of Young Albert Einstein

Albert Einstein is one of the most famous scientists of the 20th century. His ideas in the area of physics changed people's views of the world. However, when he was young, he was not considered a genius. He did not do well at school—he found it uninteresting and hated taking exams. What would his diary have been like as a 12-year-old school student? Maybe something like this …

$e=?$

$e=$

$e=m^m$

$m^c$

Munich, Germany

March 18, 1891

$e=m^2c$

Dear Diary,

School must be the most boring place on earth! I was told off so many times today in history for not concentrating. How can I concentrate when all we do is learn lists of dates by heart? We are having an exam tomorrow; I'm not looking forward to it at all. My teacher says he thinks I will fail. Unfortunately, he's probably right.

I'm going to be in a lot of trouble tomorrow, because I also have my violin lesson, and I don't know my scales. I really like violin, even though I only started because Mom said I had to. When I play, I can forget about school, and just think about the music instead.

I saw Uncle Jakob and Uncle Cäsar this week, and they are getting me interested in math and science. They show me little experiments, and it's much more interesting than the way they teach us at school. It's made me think that when I leave school, I'd like to do some sort of work with math and science. I could study the world, and find answers to things that nobody else has been able to before. That is, if I ever graduate from school. I'll have to improve my marks in history and geography first. Yuck!

Albert

$e=$

$e=2mc$

$e=mc^2$

**Answer these questions.**

1. (a) How long ago was Albert born?  _____

   (b) What was his nationality?  _____

2. (a) Highlight the things that are the same about you and Albert.

   (b) How many did you find?  _____

3. (a) Underline the things that are different about you and Albert.

   (b) How many did you find?  _____

**4.** Find evidence in the diary entry to prove the following statements. Write brief notes of the evidence you find.

   (a)  Einstein was not considered a genius at school.

   _____

   _____

   (b)  He found school uninteresting.

   _____

   _____

   (c)  Einstein became one of the most famous scientists of the 20th century.

   _____

   _____

   (d)  He hated exams.

   _____

   _____

**5.** Write what you think these people would say about Albert.

| | | |
|---|---|---|
| His schoolteacher | His violin teacher | His uncles |

**6.** What has been incorrectly written about Albert Einstein's schooldays in the passage below? Rewrite it so it is correct.

Albert Einstein was an excellent student. He concentrated hard at all times and never failed an exam. His favorite subjects were history and geography. Albert also enjoyed playing the piano.

   _____

   _____

   _____

   _____

Congratulations, Wolf. Your mission was successful.

Your next mission is to begin immediately upon receiving this document. Memorize all details, and then destroy the paper in the usual way.

1.  At 12 noon sharp, proceed to the fairground. Near the roller-coaster you will see your first contact, a woman with a buggy. She will be wearing a blue floral dress. Do not talk to her directly; instead, wait until she drops a baby bottle from the buggy. When she moves away, pick up the bottle. Inside, you will find a gold coin.

2.  Make your way directly to the fortune-telling tent. Give the gypsy woman the coin and the password "Do the bumper cars work?" She will reply, "Only on a Tuesday." She will then give you a disguise. Put this on quickly, and exit the tent at the back. BE ON YOUR GUARD. The enemy may be nearby.

3.  In the right pocket of your new disguise, you will find a key. Put it in the false sole of your shoe. Make your way to the ghost train, and get on board car number 3. Inside, you will find a wig and overcoat to change your appearance again.

4.  Get out of the ride at the end, and take the chairlift to the Ferris wheel. You will need to check the cables first—the enemy may have tampered with them. Do not look obvious as you do this. Maintain your anonymity.

5.  Near the Ferris wheel, you will see a ticket booth with a locked door. There will be no one inside. Pretend to take a stone out of your shoe, and retrieve the key. Use it to unlock the door of the booth.

6.  Inside, you will find the decoder. Hide it inside your coat. As you step out of the booth, be alert for a man in a rabbit suit. We have inside information that this is an enemy spy. Avoid him at all costs.

7.  Wander over to the clowns. Agent 12 will be in charge of the stall. Double-check by giving him the secret handshake. Put the decoder into clown number 4's mouth.

8.  Leave the fairground. After disposing of all items you collected, take whatever means of transportation you can to the airport for your flight to Istanbul.

The enemy will be watching. Good luck, Wolf.

## Answer these questions.

**1.** Before you can complete your mission, you have to make sure you understand the meaning of all the secret agent words in the instructions. Write the word that matches each meaning below.

   (a) a secret word or phrase _____

   (b) to change your appearance _____

   (c) interfered with _____

   (d) keeping your identity secret _____

   (e) something used to work out a code _____

**2.** The document says to destroy the paper in the usual way!
How might a secret agent do this?

_____

_____

**3.** On your flight to Istanbul, you complete a report to prove your mission was successful.
Write your information here.

- List some of the ways you kept the enemy from finding out about your mission.

  _____

  _____

  _____

- What items did you have to dispose of before you left the fairground?

  _____

  _____

- On the map provided, trace the path you took, and write or draw what you found at each location.

# Snakes and First Aid

We think of snakes as long, scary, scaly, poisonous creatures that slither silently along the ground waiting to pounce on us and bite! Well, not all of that is true. Snakes are not normally aggressive. They tend to bite only when they feel threatened or are mishandled. Snakes would much rather be left alone. Not all snakes have a poisonous bite. For example, the carpet snake is not venomous, while the taipan and tiger snake are very poisonous.

These are some things you can do to help prevent snakebite:
· Be noisy when walking in the bush.
· Don't wear bare feet or thongs in places snakes could be present.
· Don't put your hands in hollow logs or under piles of wood or rubbish.
· Look carefully when walking through thick grass.
· Keep sheds free of mice.
· Keep grass short around houses and playgrounds.

If you or someone you are with is unlucky enough to be bitten by a snake, here is a procedure for what to do.

1. Check there is no danger to yourself before helping the victim.
2. Check for some or all of the following symptoms or signs. They can occur 15 minutes to 2 hours after the bite (if from a poisonous snake).
   · headache
   · double vision
   · pain or tightness in chest or abdomen
   · reddening
   · puncture marks or fang scratches
   · drowsiness
   · giddiness
   · sweating
   · breathing difficulties
   · nausea and/or vomiting and diarrhea
   · swelling of bitten area
3. Rest and reassure the casualty. You may not know if the snakebite was poisonous or not at this stage.
4. Apply a pressure bandage over the bitten area and around the limb. Use a 15-cm wide bandage if available, or pantyhose or strips of material if not. The bandage keeps the limb from moving and restricts the blood from flowing freely and carrying the poison around the body.
5. Seek medical aid immediately.

These are some things you must NOT do:
· Don't wash the venom off the skin, this can help identify the type of snake so the correct antivenin can be given.
· Don't cut, squeeze or try to suck out the venom from the wound.
· Don't try to catch the snake as you may get bitten too. Do try to remember what it looked like.
· Don't use a bandage that is too constrictive or tight.

## Answer these questions.

**1.** Highlight the true facts in paragraph one.

**2.** What do you think the word "antivenin" means?

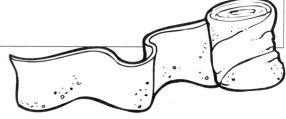

_____

_____

**3.** Briefly explain why these things are good ideas in helping prevent snakebite.

(a) being noisy in the bush

_____

_____

_____

(b) keeping grass short

_____

_____

_____

(c) keeping sheds free of mice

_____

_____

_____

(d) wearing shoes and jeans

_____

_____

_____

**4.** The passage can be divided into subheadings. Write key words and phrases to summarize the information in each section.

| Introduction–what are snakes like? | Preventing snakebites |
|---|---|
| | |
| What you should do for a snakebite victim. | What you shouldn't do for a snakebite victim. |
| | |

**5.** Check true or false.

|  | True | False |
|---|---|---|
| (a) All snakes are poisonous. | | |
| (b) Thongs are good footwear in the bush. | | |
| (c) A tiger snake is a venomous snake. | | |
| (d) Symptoms from snakebites occur immediately. | | |
| (e) A firm pressure bandage is necessary. | | |

# Prehistoric Camp

Imagine yourself in prehistoric times. You are a caveman or cavewoman, and you are going on a weekend Prehistoric Camp. Upon arriving at the campsite, you are handed this timetable for the first day.

## CAMP SCHEDULE FOR Saturday, September 18, 100,000 BC

| | | |
|---|---|---|
| 7 a.m. | Meet and grunt with all tribes in eating cave. | |
| 7:30 a.m. | **Breakfast:** | Bowl of Stegosaurus scales or miniature dinosaur eggs (plain or mud-colored). Served with Mammoth milk. |
| | | Black tar spread or sweetened paste of jungle berries on volcano-baked cave bread. |
| | | Choice of jungle fruit juice. |
| 8:30 a.m. | Chisel stone name badges with Ned Neanderthal. | |
| 9:30 a.m. | Find caves to sleep in, unpack furs, clubs and spears. | |
| 10:30 a.m. | Cavepeople sports: hard tyrannosaurus egg supplied. Note: No clubbing allowed. | |
| 12:00 | **Lunch:** | Rex Rolls |
| | | (Freshly minced Tyrannosaurus Rex, wrapped in paperbark, with dinosaur dipping sauce.) |
| | | Ice Age Mammoth Milk (Frozen mammoth milk topped with melted mud.) |
| 1:30 p.m. | Lecture: "Cooking with fire—is it for you?" or "Spears—the new-age weapon." | |
| 3:00 p.m. | Choice of activities for this afternoon—pterodactyl watching, tug of war, fur sewing | |
| 5:30 p.m. | Hunt for dinner—first caveperson to capture a plateosaurus wins a year's supply of clubs. | |
| 6:30 p.m. | Compulsory: Cavemen and women clean up (uggh soap!). | |
| 7:30 p.m. | Assemble in eating cave for dinner. | |
| | **Dinner:** | Plateosaurus Pie |
| | | (Chopped plateosaurus and tropical yellow fruit, on a base of flat cave bread and dinosaur blood, topped with melted yellow lava.) |
| 9.00 p.m. | Casino Caveman (Prehistoric Bingo). | |
| 10.30 p.m. | Retire to cave and dream of sabre-toothed tiger hunt. | |

## Answer these questions.

**1.** In the afternoon, you have a choice of activities. Highlight the choices.

**2.** Circle the activity that all campers must do.

Do you think they'd enjoy this activity? _____

Underline the words that tell you this.

**3.** For each of the prehistoric foods in the timetable, write its modern equivalent.

| Prehistoric | Modern |
|---|---|
| (a) Stegosaurus scales | Cornflakes |
| (b) Miniature dinosaur eggs | |
| (c) Black tar spread | |
| (d) Paste of jungle berries | |
| (e) Rex rolls | |
| (f) Ice-Age Mammoth Milk with melted mud | |
| (g) Plateosaurus Pie | |

**4.** Besides eating, which activity do you think you'd enjoy doing the most? Why?

_____

_____

_____

_____

**5.** (a) At what time could you watch flying dinosaurs?

_____

(b) How long do you have to unpack?

_____

(c) When can you learn about cooking?

_____

(d) What could you do to win a prize?

_____

_____

(e) What activity do you do to help identify each other more easily?

_____

**6.** Which modern sport do you think is described in the timetable?

_____

# Brief History of Flight

For thousands of years people have dreamed of being able to fly. Around the beginning of the last millennium, many people attempted to fly by strapping "wings" or kite-like machines to various parts of their bodies. They would launch themselves from high places—often resulting in their death.

Around 1500, the Italian inventor, Leonardo da Vinci, designed an ornithopter. This was a flying machine with wings designed to flap like those of a bird. Other far-sighted men also produced interesting designs, but the technology at the time couldn't bring them to life.

The world's first manned flight occurred in a hot-air balloon designed by two French brothers—the Montgolfiers—in 1783. The balloon drifted across Paris for about 25 minutes before landing safely.

In the early 1800s, an English inventor, George Cayley, founded the science of aerodynamics. After designing several models he built the first successful manned glider in 1849. It proved that the wings were "lifted" by air.

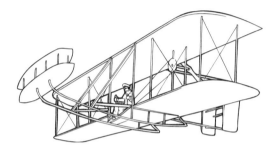

The first to fly a powered, controllable, heavier-than-air aircraft were the Wright brothers from America in 1903. The plane, piloted by Wilbur Wright, stayed in the air for 12 seconds. From then on, the Wright brothers and other inventors continued to improve airplane design and in so doing made flying more popular.

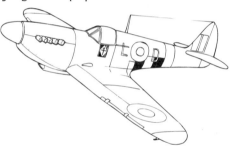

World War I (1914–1918) through to the end of World War II (1939–1945) saw a rapid advancement in airplane design and engineering improvements. Aircraft became larger, faster, more maneuverable and reliable, as well as being able to carry heavier loads.

The development of the jet engine towards the end of World War II enabled large planes to travel long distances at high speeds. The world has become much smaller with the opportunity of continually more accessible overseas travel.

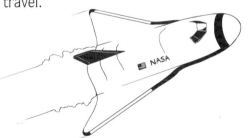

Aircraft have been designed to travel to outer space. Rockets took astronauts to the moon and back in the late 1960s and early 1970s. The first space shuttle, *Columbia*, was launched in 1981. Space shuttles take off like a rocket and land like an airplane. They can be re-used many times, making space travel far less expensive.

Today, the diversity of aircraft is enormous. There are gliders, helicopters, seaplanes, stealth fighters, jumbo jets, ultralight planes and special purpose planes such as those for crop-dusting farming areas, to name just a few. How many others can you think of?

## Answer these questions.

**1.** Highlight each inventor and nationality in a different color.

**2.** Circle all the different types of flying machines found in the report.

**3.** (a)  Explain what this person is doing.

_____

_____

(b)  Do you think he is foolish or brave? Why?

_____

_____

_____

**4.** The two World Wars brought rapid advancement in airplane technology.

Why do you think this was, and what were the advancements?_____

_____

_____

_____

**5.** Complete the time line.

| DATE | EVENT |
|------|-------|
| 1500 | _____ |
|      | _____ |
| 1783 | _____ |
| _____ | George Cayley builds the first successful manned glider. |
| _____ | The Wright brothers fly a powered aircraft. |
| _____ | Development of the jet engine. |
| 1960s | _____ |
| 1981 | _____ |

**6.** What do you think was the most important flying invention? Give a reason.

_____

_____

_____

# Haunted or Harmless?

You are a journalist, and your boss has sent you to a small town to investigate a phone call made to your office. The caller claimed that the old Tower Hotel is haunted. You meet the caller, Mrs. Sandra Jackson, at a coffee shop. Here is what she says:

"Last night was the most frightening night of my life. After arriving at the hotel, I was tired, so I went to bed early. As soon as I shut my eyes, I could feel the room shaking. Everything on the shelves started to rattle. Not long after, a horrible wailing, shrieking sound awoke me—it was inhuman. To top it off, my door, which was locked, suddenly opened, then slammed shut, as though someone had entered my room. I packed my bags as fast as I could, and went to another hotel. Make sure you write this all down in your newspaper. I want the truth told."

You decide to interview the hotel manager, Mr. Scott Sanderson, for his side of the story. After hearing Mrs. Jackson's complaints, he says:

"I'm sorry that Mrs. Jackson was frightened last night, but I believe there is a normal explanation for everything. About 7 p.m. last night, our elevators broke down, and we decided to get them fixed right away. Due to the equipment the workers used, there was some shaking that occurred for a short time throughout the hotel. The sound she heard was probably the young boy staying in the room next to her, who was practising his violin for a competition. Unfortunately, we have thin walls at this hotel.

"As for her door opening and closing, many guests often confuse someone else's room for their own, and instead of apologizing, they just shut the door again. Mrs. Jackson probably forgot to lock her door. Please print my explanations in your paper—this hotel may be old, but it is not haunted."

## Answer these questions.

**1.** Mrs. Jackson used many words and phrases that show strong feelings compared to Mr. Sanderson. List some of these below.

_____

_____

**2.** Do you think Mrs. Jackson might change her mind after she heard Mr. Sanderson's version?

Why/Why not? _____

_____

**3.** What do you think really happened that night?

_____

_____

_____

**4.** Write your report for the newspaper based on what you think happened. You will need to include a catchy headline. Also make sure your report answers the questions – "who?," "what?," "when?," "why?" and "how?"

**5.** Complete the missing information.

| What Mrs. Jackson experienced | Mr. Sanderson's explanation |
|---|---|
| (a) room shaking | |
| (b) wailing sound | |
| (c) locked door opening | |
| (d) door slamming | |

 # Channel 16 News Report

Kim Spencer
(Channel 16 News)

Imagine you turn on your television to Channel 16, and you see a news reporter, speaking to you live from the scene of a rowdy demonstration:

"I'm standing out the front of the Fox and Black Cereal Company, where a crowd of over 1,000 people has been protesting for more than two hours at the company's refusal to give out any prizes won in their recent "Treasure" competition.

The company advertised that 500 boxes of their cereal contained a plastic gold coin, and lucky customers who found a coin could claim a money prize according to its value, which ranged from $50 to $5,000.

But Fox and Black were horrified last week when thousands of excited people rang them to claim prizes. It has since been discovered that every box of cereal sold in the last month has contained a gold coin. The company has claimed it cannot afford this and has refused to pay any money at all, saying that the competition was sabotaged. It has taken all remaining boxes of cereal from supermarket shelves, and said that this is all it can do.

But the angry protestors around me say they are not giving up without a fight. They say they won their money fair and square. We are waiting for the company president, Mr. Ron Thompson, to appear so he can give his comments on the situation, but it is doubtful if he will come out and face this furious crowd. The leader of the protest, Mr. Sam Michaels, has just told me that the protestors will camp here for weeks if necessary, until someone will talk to them.

I'll be back with more soon. This is Kim Spencer, live from Fox and Black, signing off for Channel 16 News."

**Answer these questions.**

1. Find the word in the report which means:

   (a) Noisy                                             _____

   (b) Firmly said no                                    _____

   (c) A gathering to show support for an issue          _____

   (d) A group of people making a strong complaint       _____

   (e) Damaged on purpose                                _____

2. Highlight three words that describe the feelings of the company, the customers or the protestors.

**3.** Fox and Black claim that their competition was sabotaged. Who could have done this, and why?

_____

_____

_____

_____

_____

**4.** Ron Thompson eventually decides to talk to the crowd. Write what he might say in the speech balloon, and then what Sam Michaels might reply in the other speech balloon.

**5.** The next day, this story is reported in the newspaper. Write a suitable headline.

_____

Reading for Detail – Book 2 World Teachers Press®

# The Egg and Bottle Experiment

This amazing experiment you will learn to perform is all to do with air pressure. Air pressure is a powerful force. When you swim underwater you can feel water pushing on your body. The air all around you does the same. However, your body is used to it so you don't notice. The pressure is caused by a layer of air called the atmosphere, which surrounds the Earth. This layer extends to about five kilometers above the Earth's surface.

When an astronaut comes back to Earth after a space trip where there is no atmosphere (or air pressure)—he or she can feel the air pressure until the body gets used to it once more.

Now for the experiment!

## You will need:

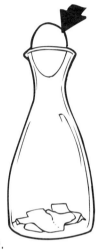

- a hard-boiled egg without the shell
- a bottle with a neck slightly smaller than the egg
- a piece of paper
- a match

## Method

1. Check that the egg will sit firmly in the neck of the bottle.
2. Tear the paper into strips and put them into the bottle.
3. Light the paper by dropping a burning match into the bottle.
4. Quickly sit the egg on the neck of the bottle.

   Astonishingly, you will see the egg being sucked into the bottle with a gurgle and a pop!

## How it works

As the paper burns, it uses up all the oxygen in the air. The egg has sealed the neck of the bottle so no more air can get inside. This reduces the air pressure inside the bottle and—presto!—the egg is sucked in. (In fact, the outside air pressure *pushes* the egg into the bottle.)

**Answer these questions.**

**1.** Highlight the sentence that explains why …

   (a) we don't feel air pressure.

   (b) an astronaut returning to Earth can feel the pressure.

**2.** Circle five verbs in the method section.

**3.** Complete the procedure for the egg and bottle experiment.

**Title**
Name of
experiment
_____

**Aim**
What is
the experiment
trying to show?
_____

_____

_____

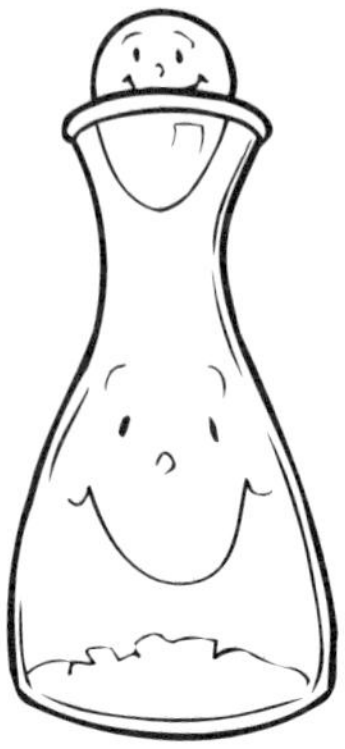

**Steps to follow**
_____

_____

_____

_____

_____

_____

_____

**Results**
What happened?

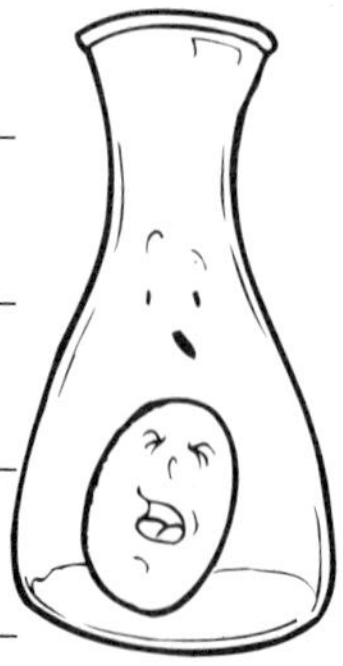

**Explanation**
How did it work?

_____        _____

_____        _____

_____        _____

**4.** What do you think would happen if …

(a) you didn't take the shell off the egg?

_____

(b) you used a wide-necked bottle?

_____

(c) you didn't put the egg quickly onto the neck of the bottle?

_____

# The Shaky Hand Game

You actually need a steady hand rather than a shaky one to be a winner in this game! The game is based on a simple electrical circuit. The circuit is powered by a battery, which provides a small, safe amount of electricity. Now for the instructions!

## Equipment

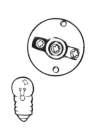

a 9-volt battery    a 9-volt bulb and a bulb holder    30-amp fuse wire    lightweight electric cord    cardboard box with a lid, scissors, ruler, pencil and screwdriver

## Instructions

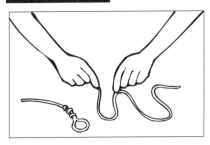
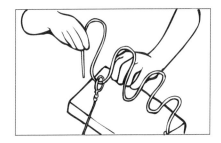
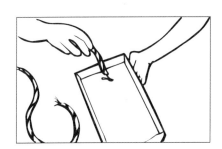

1. You need a piece of fuse wire 15 cm long and another 40 cm. Make a loop at one end of the 15-cm piece. Curve the long wire into a wavy shape.

2. Thread the long piece of wire through the loop. With a pencil, make two holes in the lid of the box. Push the ends of the wavy wire through the holes.

3. Now cut the electric cord into a 55-cm length and two 20-cm lengths. After stripping the ends, join one end of a 20-cm length to the end of the wavy wire.

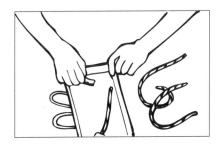
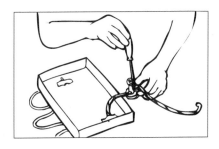
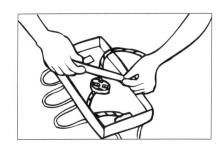

4. Securely tape both ends of the wavy wire to the inside of the box lid.

5. Now screw the bulb to its holder and attach the two 20-cm lengths of electric cord to the bulb holder.

6. Make a hole to push the bulb through the lid. Attach it securely.

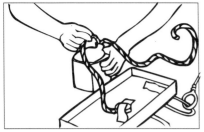
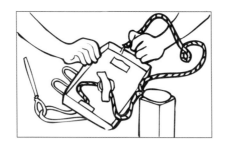
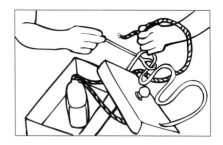

7.  Join the free length of the electric cord to the battery. Now attach one end of the 55-cm length to the other battery terminal.

8.  Push the free end of the 55-cm length through a hole made in a corner of the lid.

9.  Finally, join the end of the wire loop to the 55-cm length and close the box!

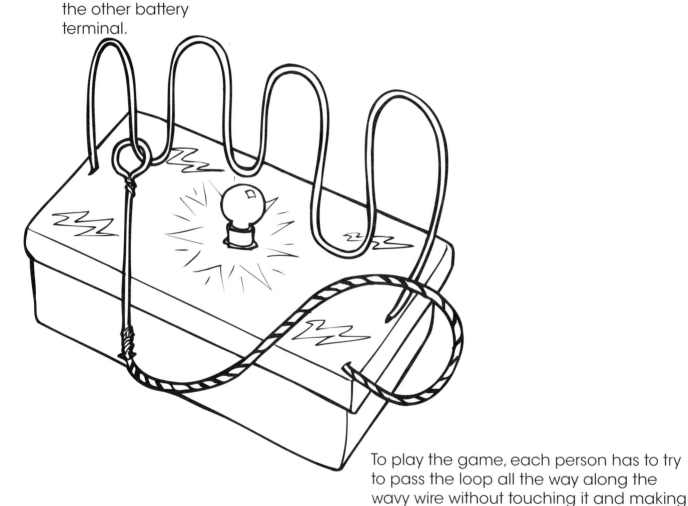

To play the game, each person has to try to pass the loop all the way along the wavy wire without touching it and making the light go on. The more bends you make in the wire, the harder the game is to play.

## How it works

The light goes on when everything is joined together to make a simple electrical circuit, or a complete circle for electricity to go around. Electricity runs from the battery, to the bulb, then back to the battery. The light will stay off if you keep the circuit "broken" by not letting the loop touch the wavy wire.

How shaky is your hand?

**Answer these questions.**

**1.** Think of another suitable name for the game.

_____

**2.** What do you think would happen if:

(a) the connections became loose?

_____

_____

(b) you didn't strip the ends of the electric cord?

_____

_____

**3.** Why do you think the game is harder to play if there are more bends in the wire?

_____

_____

**4.** After you screw the bulb into the holder and attach the two pieces of electric cord, what is the next step?

_____

_____

**5.**

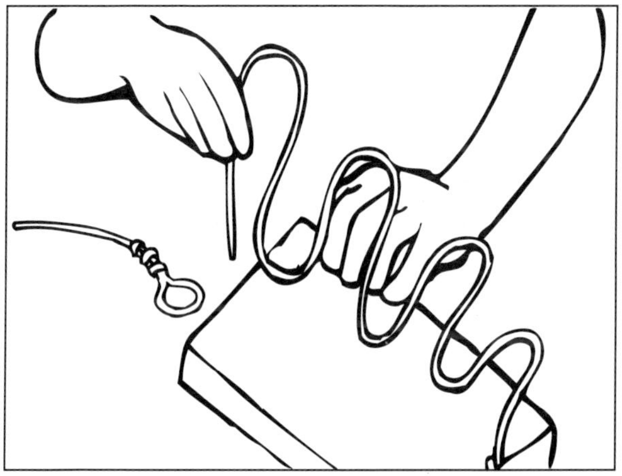

This person is trying to follow step 2. What has he/she done wrong?

_____

_____

_____

_____

_____

**6.** (a) Explain what an electrical circuit is in your own words.

_____

_____

_____

_____

_____

(b) What happens if the electrical circuit is completed during the game?

_____

_____

_____

_____

_____

_____

# A Dream Holiday?

The Cheapannasty Travel Agency is desperately trying to get tourists to visit the La Noxious holiday resort it recently picked up at a very low price. Here is a description of the resort:

The resort is found in a stormy, wet, isolated location and consists of a group of old, dilapidated chalets with one shared toilet and bathroom. The chalets overlook a crocodile-filled river and a mosquito-infested swamp. During the day, you can smell the pollution pouring from a nearby factory and listen to the horrible sound of crows. At night it is bitterly cold, and there is no wood to put in the cracked old fireplace.

For entertainment, you can walk along a beach covered with rocks, visit a boring museum featuring postage stamps or have dinner in a tiny dining room which serves sausages for dinner every night.

A creative advertising executive, however, came up with the following description of the resort to put in a glossy brochure:

> Looking for your dream holiday? Escape to our tropical hideaway.
>
> Discover old-fashioned charm with our rustic chalets, decorated in the style of yesteryear. Enjoy the company of your neighbors every day, or sit back and relax as you catch glimpses of fascinating creatures as old as time just outside your window. Each chalet overlooks the water, which literally swarms with wildlife.
>
> In the morning, take a deep breath of the thickly-scented air, as the native bird life croons its special song; and at night, sit around our antique fireplace, and bring your family closer together.
>
> There's so much to do! Why not explore our unique beach, discover the town's fascinating philatelic history, or have a sumptuous sizzling feast at our quaint, cosy restaurant?
>
> Paradise awaits you—BOOK TODAY!

**Answer these questions.**

1. Find these words in the text and explain what you think the word means. Then write a dictionary meaning to check your answer.

| Word | My meaning | Dictionary meaning |
|---|---|---|
| rustic | | |
| philatelic | | |
| sumptuous | | |
| dilapidated | | |
| antique | | |

**2.** The advertisement stretches the truth about what the resort is really like. Complete the table below about the descriptions.

| Brochure's description | Actual description |
|---|---|
| | stormy and wet |
| rustic chalets | |
| | crocodile-filled river |
| | mosquito-infested |
| crooning native birds | |
| thickly-scented air | |
| antique fireplace | |
| unique beach | |
| | postage stamp museum |
| quaint, cosy restaurant | |
| sizzling feast | |

**3.** Would you like to visit the resort if you'd only read the glossy brochure? _____

Why/Why not? _____

_____

_____

_____

**4.** The Cheapannasty Travel Agency decides not to use the brochure. It is to be changed to advertise the resort as an adventure holiday rather than a dream holiday. You are hired for the job. Write your ad using the first description.

**Pages 6–7: The Trojan Horse**

1.  Teacher check

2.  (a) Trojan
    (b) Greek

3.  greatest, mighty, colossal, great, huge, massive

4.  Teacher check

5.  Helen was so beautiful the Greeks sent a fleet of 1,000 ships to bring her back.

6.  (a) The hurt or damage done to pay back for the bad things done to you.
    (b) King Menelaus declaring war on Troy after his wife Helen left him for Paris, Greeks massacring the Trojans and burning the city after capturing Troy.

7.  Teacher check

**Pages 8–9: The Elephant's Child**

1.  "Come close," said the crocodile, "and I'll tell you."

2.  swat insects, pick up things to eat, throw mud over himself; teacher check

3.–5. Teacher check

**Pages 10–11: April Fools' Feast**

1.  (a) fact
    (b) opinion
    (c) fact
    (d) opinion
    (e) fact

2.  Teacher check

3.  She was tired of eating the same healthy food all the time./It was April Fools' Day

4.–5. Teacher check

6.

| Real food | Trick food |
|---|---|
| ice cream | mashed potato |
| chocolate topping | gravy |
| candy bar and cookie crumbs | fish stick |

7.  (a) lurking
    (b) fool
    (c) topping
    (d) healthy

**Pages 12–13: Winning Isn't Everything**

1.  "Her expression quickly charges to a smile."

2.–5. Teacher check

**Pages 14–16: The Clock Struck**

1.  TOM    Hey, what's going on?
    SALLY    Tom, stop fooling around.
    TOM    I can't help it.

2.–5. Teacher check

6.  To add atmosphere and suspense to the play.

**Pages 17–18: Animal Camouflage**

1.  Teacher check

2.  (a) predators
    (b) lioness
    (c) harmful, poisonous
    (d) dim
    (e) camouflaged
    (f) dawn

3.–5. Teacher check

**Pages 19–20: Carnivorous Plant Facts**

1.  These plants attract, capture, kill and digest animal life forms.

2.  They digest their prey by the use of special enzymes.

3.  Teacher check

4.  A pitcher is a large jug for holding fluids. A pitcher plant has a trumpet-shaped "jug" for collecting rainwater.

5.  (a) sour – sweet
    (b) herbivore – carnivore
    (c) release – capture
    (d) repel – attract

6.  Teacher check

**Pages 21–22: A Snack for Shannon**

1.–4. Teacher check

5.  (a) iii         (b) ii

**Pages 23–24: Helping Mom and Dad**

1.–2. Teacher check

3.  She was worried other people might think they were strange and tease Brett, she didn't feel well with a splitting headache, Brett's father was rundown.

4.  Teacher check

5.  (a) heavily; Teacher check
    (b) splitting; Teacher check
    (c) good; Teacher check
    (d) softly; Teacher check

6.  Teacher check

**Pages 25–26: Bull Ant Bulletin**

1. Teacher check

2. (a) thousands
   (b) teenage, unthinking
   (c) well-known
   (d) hospital, overflowing

3.–5. Teacher check

**Pages 27–28: Deluxe Dinner Parties**

1.–5. Teacher check

**Pages 29–30: The Secret Diary of the Monster in the Bedroom**

1. Left some candy for the little girl, made some clown shadows.

2.–4. Teacher check

**Pages 31–32: Diary of Young Albert Einstein**

1. (a) Year – 1879
   (b) German

2.–6. Teacher check

**Pages 33–34: Top Secret—For Your Eyes Only**

1. (a) password
   (b) disguise
   (c) tampered
   (d) maintaining your anonymity
   (e) decoder

2.–3. Teacher check

**Pages 35–36: Snakes and First Aid**

1. Teacher check

2. An injection to fight the venom from a spider or snake.

3. (a) Being noisy—snakes will hear your approach and get out of your way.
   (b) Short grass—nowhere for snakes to hide for protection.
   (c) Sheds free of mice—snakes won't be attracted to shed to catch mice to eat.
   (d) Shoes and jeans provide protection for your skin from bites.

4. Teacher check

5. (a) false
   (b) false
   (c) true
   (d) false
   (e) true

**Pages 37–38: Prehistoric Camp**

1. Attend a lecture, pterodactyl watching, tug of war, fur sewing

2. Compulsory: Cavemen and women clean up (Uggh soap!)

3.–4. Teacher check

5. (a) 3:00 p.m.
   (b) One hour
   (c) 1:30 p.m.
   (d) Capture a plateosaurus
   (e) Chisel stone name badges

**Pages 39–40: Brief History of Flight**

1. Leonardo da Vinci – Italian
   George Cayley – English
   Montgolfier brothers – French
   Wright brothers – American

2. kite-like machines, ornithopter, hot-air balloon, glider, heavier-than-air aircraft, jet, rocket, space shuttle, helicopter, seaplane, stealth fighter, jumbo jet, ultralight planes

3. Teacher check

4. (a) During the two World Wars a lot of time, effort and money was put into airplane technology as aircraft were an important part of the Wars.
   (b) Aircraft became larger, faster, more maneuverable and reliable and able to carry heavier loads.

5. **1500** – Leonardo da Vinci designed the ornithopter
   **1783** – first manned flight occurred in a hot-air balloon
   1849 – **George Cayley builds the first successful manned glider**
   1903 – **The Wright Brothers fly a powered aircraft**
   1944/45 – **Development of the jet engine**
   **1960s** – rockets took astronauts to the moon
   **1981** – The first space shuttle was launched

6. Teacher check

**Pages 41–42: Haunted or Harmless?**

1.–4. Teacher check

5. (a) The workers were fixing the elevator.
   (b) Young boy practising his violin.
   (c) Mrs. Sanderson forgot to lock her door.
   (d) Guest opening her door by mistake.

**Pages 43–44: Channel 16 News Report**

1. (a) rowdy
   (b) refused
   (c) demonstration
   (d) protestors
   (e) sabotaged

2. horrified, excited, angry, furious

3.–5. Teacher check

**Pages 45–46: The Egg and Bottle Experiment**

1.  (a) "However, your body is used to it, so you don't notice."

    (b) "When an astronaut comes back to Earth after a space trip where there is no atmosphere (or air pressure)—he or she can feel the air pressure until the body gets used to it once more."

2.  check, sit, tear, put, light, using, dropping, sucked

3.–4. Teacher check

**Pages 47–49: Shaky Hand Game**

1.  Teacher check

2.  (a) The circuit would not be complete so the light would not go on when the loop touched the wavy wire.

    (b) The plastic covering would prevent the wire under the electric cord from joining and a circuit could not be made.

3.  The more bends made, the harder it is to not touch the wavy wire.

4.  Make a small hole in the middle of the box lid, push the bulb through and tape it on the inside.

5.  Person has forgotten to thread loop onto wire.

6.  (a) Teacher check

(b) The light will come on.

**Pages 50–51: A Dream Holiday**

1.  rustic – relating to the country

    philatelic – relating to collecting and studying of postage stamps

    sumptuous – splendid or superb

    dilapidated – fallen into ruin or decay

    antique – an object of art or piece of furniture which was made long ago

2.

| Brochure's description | Actual description |
|---|---|
| tropical | **stormy and wet** |
| **rustic chalets** | dilapidated chalets |
| fascinating creatures as old as time | **crocodile-filled river** |
| swarms with wildlife | **mosquito-infested** |
| **crooning native birds** | horrible sound of crows |
| **thickly-scented air** | pollution from factory |
| **antique fireplace** | cracked old fireplace |
| **unique beach** | beach covered with rocks |
| philatelic history | **postage stamp museum** |
| **quaint, cosy restaurant** | old, tiny dining room |
| **sizzling feast** | sausages for dinner |

3.–4. Teacher check

# Books Available from World Teachers Press®

## MATH

*Essential Facts and Tables*
    Grades 3-10

*Math Puzzles Galore*
    Grades 4-8

*Practice Math*
    Grades 4, 5, 6, 7

*Math Speed Tests*
    Grades 1-3, 3-6

*Problem Solving with Math*
    Grades 2-3, 4-5, 6-8

*Math Through Language*
    Grades 1-2, 2-3, 3-4

*Exploring Measurement*
    Grades 2-3, 3-4, 5-6

*Chance, Statistics & Graphs*
    Grades 1-3, 3-5

*Step Into Tables*
    Elementary

*Problem Solving Through Investigation*
    Grades 5-8, 7-10

*The Early Fraction Book*
    Grades 3-4

*The Fraction Book*
    Grades 5-8

*It's About Time*
    Grades 2-3, 4-5

*Do It Write Math*
    Grades 2-3

*Mental Math Workouts*
    Grades 4-6, 5-7, 6-8, 7-9

*Math Grid Games*
    Grades 4-8

*High Interest Mathematics*
    Grades 5-8

*Math Homework Assignments*
    Gr. 2, 3, 4, 5, 6, 7

*Visual Discrimination*

*Active Math*

*Math Enrichment*

*Time Tables Challenges*

*30 Math Games*
    PreK-1

*Early Skills Series:*
    Addition to Five
    Counting and Recognition to Five
    Cutting Activities
    Early Visual Skills

*Spatial Relations*
    Grades 1-2, 3-4, 5-6

*High Interest Geometry*

*Money Matters*
    Grades 1, 2, 3

## LANGUAGE ARTS

*My Desktop Dictionary*
    Grades 2-5

*Spelling Essentials*
    Grades 3-10

*Reading for Detail*
    Grades 4-5, 6-7

*Writing Frameworks*
    Grades 2-3, 4-5, 6-7

*Spelling Success*
    Grades 1, 2, 3, 4, 5, 6, 7

*My Junior Spelling Journal*
    Grades 1-2

*My Spelling Journal*
    Grades 3-6

*Cloze Encounters*
    Grades 1-2, 3-4, 5-6

*Comprehension Lifters*
    1, 2, 3, 4

*Grammar Skills*
    Grades 2-3, 4-5, 6-8

*Vocabulary Development through Dictionary Skills*
    Grades 3-4, 5-6, 7-8

*Recipes for Readers*
    Grades 3-6

*Step Up To Comprehension*
    Grades 2-3, 4-5, 6-8

*Cloze*
    Grades 2-3, 4-5, 6-8

*Cloze in on Language*
    Grades 3-5, 4-6, 5-7, 6-8

*Initial Sounds Fold-Ups*

*Phonic Sound Cards*

*Early Activity Phonics*

*Activity Phonics*

*Early Phonics in Context*

*Phonics in Context*

*Build-A-Reader*

*Communicating*
    Grades 5-6

*Oral Language*
    Grades 2-3, 4-5, 6-8

*Listen! Hear!*
    Grades 1-2, 3-4, 5-6

*Phonic Fold-Ups*

*Classical Literature*
    Grades 2-3, 4-5, 6-8

*High Interest Vocabulary*
    Grades 5-8

*Literacy Lifters*
    1, 2, 3 ,4

*Look! Listen! Think!*
    Grades 2-3, 4-5, 6-7

*Teach Editing*
    Grades 2-3, 3-4, 5-6

*Proofreading and Editing*
    Grades 3-4, 4-8, 7-8

*High Interest Language*
    Grades 5-8

*Comprehend It!*
    Animal Theme, The Sea Theme,
    Weird and Mysterious Theme

*Comprehension for Young Readers*

*Language Skill Boosters*
    Grades 1, 2, 3, 4, 5, 6, 7

*Phonic Charts*

*Vocabulary Sleuths*
    Grades 5-7, 6-9

*Early Theme Series:*
    Bears, Creepy Crawlies, The Sea

*Phonics in Action Series:*
    Initial Sounds, Final Consonant
    Sounds, Initial Blends and
    Digraphs, Phonic Pictures

## OTHERS

*Ancient Egypt, Ancient Rome, Ancient Greece*
    Grades 4-7

*Australian Aboriginal Culture*
    Grades 3-4, 5-6, 7-8

*Reading Maps*
    Grades 2-3, 4-5, 6-8

*The Music Book*
    Grades 4-8

*Mapping Skills*
    Grades 2-3, 3-4, 5-6

*Introducing The Internet*

*Internet Theme Series:*
    Sea, The Solar System,
    Endangered Species

*Art Media*

Visit us at:
www.worldteacherspress.com
for further information and free
sample pages.